Mysteri

of Devon and Cornwall

Chris Moiser

C000071650

Bossiney Books
Launceston

First published 2001 by Bossiney Books
Langore, Launceston, Cornwall PL15 8LD
Reprinted 2002
ISBN 1-899383-46-8
Printed in Great Britain by R Booth (Troutbeck Press), Mabe, Cornwall

Introduction

For many years there have been regular reported sightings of exotic large cats throughout Britain. Although these are generally thought to have started with the Surrey Puma in 1963, Devon and Cornwall have had a very large number of sightings, and these now possibly exceed those in the rest of the country.

In zoological terms the animals are called 'exotic', meaning they are not indigenous, they do not 'belong' here. In the cryptozoological world they are referred to as 'ABCs' or Alien Big Cats. The press tend to refer to them with names such as the 'Beast of Bodmin', the 'Beast of Exmoor' or the 'Wrangaton Lion'.

These names are slightly misleading, however, as any of the large cats is capable of moving at least thirty kilometres (twenty miles) in a night if it is so minded: so the 'Beast of Exmoor' one night could be on Dartmoor by first light the following morning.

The majority of the sightings do not in fact come from the moors, but from other parts of Devon and Cornwall, and occasionally from near towns and cities. The word 'beast' seems to have been first used in the early 1980s in relation to cat sightings on Exmoor. The name 'Beast of Dartmoor' seems hardly ever to be used despite repeated reports of large cats on Dartmoor and around its edges.

If we accept the existence of exotic big cats in the two counties, the first obvious question to ask is how did they come to be here? There are several possible answers, some less likely than others.

1. They are survivors from the prehistoric past. The leopard is supposed to have become extinct about 12,000 years ago, and the lynx probably 4000 years ago, although this last period is debatable. The chance of the animals having survived virtually unnoticed to the present day seems exceedingly remote.

2. They are not a species currently known to science. This could only really be true if they were the hybrid offspring of domestic cats which had returned to the wild (become 'feral') and either European (Scottish) Wildcats or some small introduced exotic cat.

3. The animals were released from captivity. There are a number of possible types and periods of release.

(a) They escaped from travelling circuses and menageries from the 1800s onwards. This is quite possible if you look at the numbers of such enterprises and the quality of the roads on which they travelled. We know that a lion was released for malicious reasons from Ballard's menagerie in 1816. The animal attacked a horse pulling the Exeter mail coach and was recaptured shortly afterwards. Bostock's menagerie in the 1890s nearly lost their leopards when a wagon toppled over against a hedge whilst coming down the hill on the Looe road just outside Hessenford.

(b) They escaped during the 1960s and early 1970s when it was particularly easy to purchase exotic cats and there were few constraints on keeping large carnivores. They could have escaped from private and public collections or whilst in transit.

(c) They were released during or shortly after 1976, when the Dangerous Wild Animals Act came into force. This story is especially liked by the press, because it supplies a short and neat answer. It is rather a simplified explanation, though, that doesn't stand up too well to detailed examination. It certainly does not explain all the sightings in the mid 1960s.

(d) Animals were deliberately released at some point in time either for game control reasons or as part of a secret scientific experiment to see if they could adapt to the environment and establish themselves. Whilst this theory seems ludicrous to many people, it must be remembered that it was not an offence to release non-native animals into the wild in England and Wales until 1981, and in the Victorian period the Acclimatisation Society attempted to introduce many foreign species here.

4. They are non-physical entities. This is an idea I have heard on at least one occasion. Some people believe they are the ghosts of exotic cats that died in the area in the past and could not settle, possibly because they were so far from their home lands.

If we analyse the reports from eye witnesses we seem to come up with three main descriptions of the cats that have been seen: large long-tailed brown, large long-tailed black and, less commonly, medium short-tailed brown. Working through the descriptions,

Leopard cat

they seem to be identified most obviously as puma, black leopard (or panther) and lynx. However we also know that leopard cats (a cat with leopard-like spots, but only the size of a domestic cat) and jungle cats have been loose in England and Wales too. Possibly because of their size, they are seen less often and so there are fewer reports, or they may be mistaken for domestic cats or foxes.

The puma comes from the Americas, and in zoological terms is the largest of the small cats. It has a reputation for being very secretive, and the authorities in some North American states which thought they had been without pumas for over a hundred years have just discovered they are still around. Pumas typically feed on deer, and it was this lack of prey in states such as Maine that made the authorities believe the cat was extinct. It is likely that the pumas moved on to smaller game to survive as the deer became extinct.

A black variety of puma has been recorded in the wild in South and Central America, but these are phenomenally rare. There are

Puma

certainly no records of black pumas ever having been imported into Europe, and no records of a black puma ever having been caught alive. Despite these well-known facts, there are still reports of 'black pumas' having been seen in Devon and Cornwall.

The leopard comes from Africa and Asia. Although its range has been reduced considerably in the last hundred years, it is thought to be regaining some of its lost territory and learning to live alongside people on the outskirts of some African cities. Indeed they are venturing into the heavily populated areas at night.

Zoologists tend to classify cats as 'big cats' or 'small cats' on the basis of their throat structure and ability to roar. The leopard is the smallest of the big cats. Black leopards, or black panthers as they are often named, are just a black genetic form of the 'normal' leopard. They are still leopards in the same way that albino humans are still human. The rules of genetics are such that if two black leopards breed they will always produce black offspring. Black leopards do

African leopard in the wild: so far not sighted in the South West but black leopards have allegedly been seen astride branches in this position in Cornwall

occur and survive naturally in the wild, but they are considerably rarer than the usual spotted leopard and seem to be restricted to deep forest.

Black leopard

Lynx

The lynx is smaller than the puma and currently exists in Europe, Asia and North America, although some of the populations in Western Europe are very small and are really only present as a result of major conservation projects. Typically lynx feed on rabbits and hares and, given the opportunity, on small deer.

The African Lynx or Caracal has been reported in Cornwall: a painting of an animal that was sighted and drawn by an artist near Common Moor on Bodmin would seem to show a caracal.

African Lynx or Caracal

Ecology

The existence of exotic cats in Devon and Cornwall should not present too much of a challenge to the local environment. It is known from fossils found in Plymouth and Torbay that there were leopards and lions living naturally in the two counties up to about 12,000 years ago. We also know from French cave paintings of this period that the leopards were spotted (France and England were of course joined at this time). Many experts think the lynx survived until about 4000 years ago.

The smaller European wild cat still hangs on in Scotland, where it is known as the Scottish wild cat. It was certainly present in the south west until the seventeenth century and possibly later. This animal has been known to cross-breed with domestic cats, so some of its genes may linger on in some of the bigger, tougher farm cats in the west country, if not as a thoroughbred wild cat.

Whilst many of the prey animals that would have been eaten by the leopards and cave lions have become extinct, they have been replaced in recent times with introduced species which make ideal large cat food. These species include several types of deer, some game birds and of course rabbits.

The ability of the larger cats to survive in the UK is easily proved. Take for example the case of Felicity, a 'Scottish puma', and that of a clouded leopard. Felicity was caught in October 1980 in a trap on a farm in Inverness-shire, after two years of sightings and livestock losses in the area. There were conflicting views on whether she had recently been released or not. She was elderly, arthritic and became tame very quickly once caged, but her first droppings in captivity contained deer and sheep remains, which would have been consistent with her having lived in the wild for some time. Needless to say no one claimed her, and she lived out her days in the Highland Wildlife Park. Even more interestingly, puma sightings continued in the area where she was caught well after her capture.

A clouded leopard, quite a specialised species from the tropics, escaped in Kent in 1975, and was shot nine months later having fed on rabbits and lambs in the meantime. The body was that of a well-nourished and fit animal.

There are numerous other reports of leopards and pumas having escaped and then being recaptured or shot within hours, so they probably would not have had chance to catch a 'wild meal'. The leopard that escaped in Plymouth in 1968 is a typical example. The animal was in transit, and escaped from a box in a lorry parked in Plymouth Zoo overnight. When it was discovered missing the following morning, the police were called and a search ensued. It was found a small distance away, and was shot by zoo staff who deemed it too dangerous to try to capture it alive.

If animals such as the puma and the clouded leopard can survive in Scotland and Kent, then with the potential food that is present in Devon and Cornwall there is the possibility of a large exotic population.

The evidence for the presence of smaller exotic cats is even greater. Nationally a number of smaller cats have been found, including two jungle cats – one at Hayling Island and one at Ludlow – and several leopard cats. The *Western Morning News* of 21 April 1988 reported the shooting of a leopard cat at a farm near Widecombe-in-the-Moor in Devon. It had apparently been chasing a farmer's geese. Although other papers at the time reported the story well (and it even made the front page with one national paper), none were able to establish how it came to be at liberty in Devon. The explanation came several years later, in Jonathan Downes' book, *The Smaller Mystery Carnivores of the West Country*.

Jonathan had spoken to someone involved in the operation who revealed that at some time in 1987 the police had raided the home of a local drug dealer and petty criminal who, illegally, was keeping a pair of leopard cats. During the raid the animals were accidentally released. The male was the animal shot and reported in early 1988, but the female was never caught. Clearly this animal was at liberty with the male for long enough for there to have been kittens, but there have not as yet been further reports of any leopard cats in the area.

In fact the sighting of an animal like a leopard cat would not now raise an enormous amount of interest, because in recent years a new variety of domestic cat – the 'Bengal' or 'Bengali' – has been created. It is a hybrid between a leopard cat and a domestic cat that was originally bred in captivity to give the tame domestic cat a leopard cat's spots.

A similar cross has been achieved between a domestic cat and a jungle cat. This is called a 'chaussie' from the Latin name for the jungle cat, *Felis chaus*, and was bred for its size and character. Both of these hybrids are very valuable and so anyone who loses one is likely to make great efforts to get it back.

Karl Shuker, a Midlands-based cryptozoologist, has a stuffed jungle cat. It had been knocked down near Ludlow, and he believes the animal may have fathered kittens to a farm cat in the area before being killed. One kitten in particular, called Jasper, had the appearance of the chaussie.

Normally it would be unlikely for any hybrid to be formed in the wild from a domestic cat, and, say an escaped female leopard cat.

The different species would not get close enough to each other, nor would their natural behaviour encourage cross-breeding. Despite this, there is one lone hybrid cat in the world – the Kellas cat – that appears to have occurred naturally. It is a big black cat, larger than the domestic cat, and is thought to be a cross between a domestic cat and a European wild cat.

The Kellas cat was found in Scotland and has been extensively studied by the naturalist Di Francis, who at one stage kept several of them. There is some variation between individuals of this type of cat, and it seems that this may be due to how many domestic cat and wildcat genes there are in each animal.

Similar looking large black cats were reported by Hope Bourne in her book *Living on Exmoor* as inhabiting the Room Hill area of Exmoor until World War I. Whether they were hybrids, either of the Kellas type, or of some other sort, has never been established, but the possibility should be considered, particularly as there is great uncertainty about when the European wild cat died out in the area.

In considering the ecological consequences of exotic cats in Devon and Cornwall, it is necessary to include the lion, as there have been numerous alleged sightings at Wrangaton and Bittaford in Devon.

Lions are somewhat different from other members of the cat family in that they are social cats, normally living in a family group. All the other cats tend to lead a solitary life, except when breeding or when rearing cubs. Lions can survive on their own, but this is rare. Also, because of their larger size they eat considerably more than a leopard or a puma does. Accordingly they are less likely to subsist on rabbits or small deer. The typical prey would be sheep, pigs or cows. This would obviously make them more likely to be noticed by the local farmers and the authorities. They would, because of their size, also pose a much greater risk to humans than pumas or leopards do.

The only possible explanation for a genuine sighting would be if an illegally held pet lion was to have escaped briefly and been recaptured by the owner. As ludicrous as this sounds there were two unlicensed lions living in a garage near Bodmin in 1983. They escaped on a number of occasions before being rehomed at Dartmoor Wildlife Park.

The Beast of Exmoor

The story of the beast of Exmoor starts in 1982 when a number of lambs were lost on Eric Ley's Drewstone farm near South Molton. The losses decreased and then stopped, but whether that was because he had shot several foxes or because another predator had moved on was not clear.

The following spring was even worse, with 30 lambs having been taken by 15 April. The neighbours were losing livestock as well. The attacks were also different from those normally ascribed to dogs. Lambs were taken quickly and quietly at night with little disturbance to the rest of the flock.

On 19 April the Torrington beagle pack was used to search the area, with fifty armed farmers on foot and horseback and a police helicopter in support. They found nothing, despite a daylight sheep kill being investigated. A newspaper report on the front page of a North Devon newspaper on 21 April led to national newspapers picking up the story the next day. And so the 'Beast of Exmoor' was born.

By May the situation was so bad that the Royal Marines were called in, a decision without precedent. Unfortunately for this reason it also attracted the media in large quantities, and on 7 May one national newspaper offered a reward of £1000 for the first photograph of 'the beast'. Both the Marines and the police saw this as a dangerous move, as it would inevitably attract the public into an area where there was a concentration of firearms. For safety the Marines were withdrawn, although they secretly returned on 17 May and continued their surveillance only to pull out finally in early July, admitting defeat. Whilst animals had been seen, it had not been possible to take a 'safe' shot because of the background on each occasion.

Sightings by locals continued and were of a large black cat-like animal and a large dog. Certainly dog kills of sheep had occurred and a couple of dogs were shot in the act of worrying sheep.

Following a lull in the sheep slaughters during July, they started up again in August. At this stage many suggestions were put forward about the identity of the killer, which included wolf, puma, panther and even a bear! The latter suggestion was made by an anonymous caller to an Exeter-based radio station.

Killings continued in succeeding years, but not at the initial intensity of the 1983 attacks when around eighty sheep died in ninety days. Late 1987 and early 1988 saw another flurry of media interest when Ovis Farm near Bratton Fleming lost a total of 30 lambs. The killings were on a regular basis and almost the entire corpse was eaten.

Within a week of this being reported a valuable foal was killed and partially eaten 15 km (9 miles) away, near Barnstaple. Nigel Brierley, a local naturalist who had been studying the Beast of Exmoor, was able to examine the corpse where it was found and saw footprints over 10 cm (4 inches) wide.

A subsequent post mortem suggested the animal had died of hypothermia, but this was strongly refuted by Brierley.

About this time it was also announced that Trevor Beer, another local naturalist and author of *The Beast of Exmoor – Fact or Legend*, was mapping the movements of the Exmoor Beast. In fact he had been doing so for the previous five years and had already come to the conclusion that the animal(s) spent the spring and summer on the more remote moorland, feeding on wild game. Then during the autumn and winter they were forced by the weather to move down into lower agricultural land near the coast. Brierley and Beer collaborated on many of their researches and shortly afterwards Brierley published his book *They Stalk by Night*.

One possible explanation about where the Beast of Exmoor may have come from, or more correctly, possibly where it *should* have lived, came via friends. Lyn and Danny Reynolds are the directors of Exmoor Zoological Gardens at Bratton Fleming, near Barnstaple. They acquired the site in 1993 shortly after it had ceased trading as a bird garden, and with the injection of some cash and a lot of hard work they redeveloped it into the beautiful establishment it is now.

About two years after they took over the zoo Danny telephoned me one night with an interesting story. Earlier that day he had been looking in some of the offshow outbuildings and had found a box

Dartmoor Wildlife Park owner Ellis Daw firmly believes the 'Beast of Exmoor' to be a puma. This sign is by his puma enclosure

containing documents and other items from the early days of the park's operation. There were also several cage labels. All but one related to animals which Danny knew had been exhibited at the park some time before they acquired it.

The label which did not fit with this list of previous exhibits was, significantly, for a puma cage! Enquiries with the previous owner did not supply an answer, and no one locally is aware of the park ever exhibiting pumas. The only likely explanations would be either that the label arrived there accidentally, or that at some stage in its early history the park was preparing to receive pumas, but they never arrived. Alternatively, they arrived and escaped immediately, perhaps while being transferred to their new cage.

To make it even more interesting, Danny believes the park first opened in about 1982. As with many other small animal collections, it is quite possible that various non-domestic animals were kept on the site before the opening. It is also worth mentioning that there have been several domestic livestock kills and some 'Beast of Exmoor' sightings within a few hundred metres of the collection.

Most of the sightings in the Exmoor area are of long-tailed black cats, but there are also some of puma-type animals. In addition, in the period between 1963 and 1985 Dr Frank Turk, an eminent zoologist, recorded six sightings of lynx-type cats in this area. Sightings have still continued up to the present, as have livestock kills.

The Beast of Bodmin

Compared to the other cat sightings, the 'Beast of Bodmin' appears relatively late on. The earliest reports referring to sheep kills by a big cat come from 1992. (Puma sightings were made further west in Cornwall, in St Ives, St Columb and Ladock, as early as 1966, but the livestock kills were few and they quickly stopped.)

The Bodmin story is centred around the Bolventor area and the south of the moor. Ninestones Farm at Common Moor was a particular centre of activity. Here farmer Rosemary Rhodes lost six sheep to possible cat kills in the first four months of 1992.

As time progressed further killings were reported as were odd sightings, mostly of large black cats, mainly to the south and west of the moor. Typical of such sightings is that of Michael Williams, a psychic phenomena investigator, who describes seeing a black animal that was 'too large for a cat' and 'not having the look of a dog'. It crossed the road 15 metres (16 yards) ahead of him, near St Breward, on 19 May 1993.

There followed in characteristic fashion a few quiet months and then a couple of sheep kills and some more sightings. Examination of the dead sheep led to divergent reports. A local abbatoir stated the corpse they inspected was definitely not killed by a dog, while a Ministry veterinary expert stated it *had* been attacked by a dog. During late October 1993 the story took an even odder twist when a woman walking her dog in the Cardinham area in the early hours of the morning claimed to have been attacked by a 'puma-type' animal and knocked unconscious. The attack was reported to the police who revealed there had been two sheep killings in the area during the previous five days.

In no time at all *The Sun* had published a front page news story citing the 'Beast of Bodmin' as the culprit. An accompanying photograph was taken by Colin Shepherd and showed a cat on top of a wall, possibly with the head of a cub projecting from behind the wall. It was said to have been taken at a secret location 'miles away from where the woman was knocked down last week'.

A few days later the *Western Morning News* reported a plan to place a female puma in a cage on the moor to try to lure the 'local' animal into the open. The privately-owned captive puma was from Dartmoor Wildlife Park. Caradon Council, the local authority in whose area she was to be placed, would have needed to supervise parts of the operation, but they were not particularly happy about the situation and publicly stated as much. So the story fizzled out gently when the puma was returned to the wildlife park, and *The Sun* reporter went back to London.

Back at Ninestones Farm Rosemary Rhodes had been busy with her video recorder and had produced some footage of a large black cat in a field near the farm. This footage was supplied to the BBC which produced a 'Close-up' programme on the big cat phenomena, with emphasis on the Beast of Bodmin. It was broadcast in the south-west region on 9 December, and was followed up immediately afterwards with a talkback feature on local radio. During the radio programme a number of experts suggested that the cat on Mrs Rhodes' film was either a black leopard or a puma.

One result of the film was a request from John and Robert Goodenough, neighbours of Mrs Rhodes and farmers who had also suffered serious sheep losses, that the government employ marksmen to track down and kill the cats.

The next year started well. *The Sun* again carried a story and another photograph, this time taken by Keith Farmer at Lanivet, about 24 km (15 miles) from where their previous picture had been snapped. The *Western Morning News* also ran the story and photograph on the same morning. The picture showed a silhouette-like image of a cat by a large pool. The cat had a suspiciously long tail, and its authenticity was questioned by a number of people almost immediately. At Ninestones Farm the sheep killings continued.

PC Peter Keen, a local police officer and dog-handler based at Bodmin, was so interested in the sightings that he used his leave to go on a fact-finding trip to the United States. Having had one cat sighting himself, he told the Plymouth-based *Evening Herald* that he was convinced there were several pumas on the moor, and possibly a black panther as well.

Following pressure from the farming community, in early January 1995 the junior agriculture minister, Angela Browning, announced there was to be a study over the next two months to establish whether the 'Beast' really did exist and whether it posed a risk to livestock. A sum of £8200 was allocated and two government scientists were appointed to conduct the study. It was set to last up to six months and was to include an analysis of the Rosemary Rhodes video from 1993, an assessment of plaster cast footprints and a detailed examination of five livestock kills thought to be big cat related.

Eventually the report was published on 19 July: a slight delay had occurred because the ministry could not obtain enough livestock kills to examine. The report found no verifiable evidence of the presence of any big cat but, quite correctly, stated it could not prove that a big cat was not present.

The local farming community was furious and made accusations of deliberate underfunding and total whitewashing. Whilst I agreed the study had been seriously underfunded and much longer should have been spent in acquiring evidence, I did feel the report was a logical assessment of the evidence that had been obtained and examined. The two scientists had also quite clearly recognised their own limitations in specialist areas such as footprint recognition and had formally acknowledged this.

However, their work on the visual evidence was good. For both the video footage and the Colin Shepherd photograph they visited the sites with measuring poles, and on one occasion they even recruited a passing domestic cat to show quite clearly that the animal in the video was well within the size ranges of an ordinary moggie. Several experts who had commented on the Colin Shepherd photograph and the video footage when they were first made public must have been rather embarassed. I know at least three who identified the video as 'definitely [showing] a black panther'.

Local indignation was expressed in the papers and a plan was announced by London Zoo for them to visit the area and livetrap any big cat if the funding could be raised. About two weeks later a leopard skull was found at Golitha Falls on the south of the moor. Doug Richardson, then assistant curator of mammals at London Zoo, identified it as from a cat, almost certainly a puma or a leopard. He also confirmed it smelt as if decomposition was still taking place and the animal had almost certainly died within the last year.

The skull was passed on to the Natural History Museum which issued a statement in August making it clear the skull was that of a male leopard. However they also found that the brain case contained half of a tropical cockroach egg, and there was damage at the back of the skull consistent with its preparation as a rug or hunting trophy.

In other words the animal had probably died and been mounted overseas many years previously, and therefore was a hoax. The Natural History Museum have a nice internet web site explaining how they came to their conclusions. *The Times* ran a story with the beautiful headline 'Beast of Bodmin exposed as Piltdown Puss'.

This in fact was the third skull found in Devon and Cornwall within the space of ten years. Each of them, although initially hailed as proof of pumas or leopards living in the area, was subsequently discredited. In January 1988 a big cat skull was discovered near Lustleigh on the eastern edge of Dartmoor. It was never subjected to serious scientific examination, but Dr Karl Shuker, who saw a photograph of it, was of the opinion that it may have been a leopard skull. He also expressed a view that marks on it were consistent with it having been attached to a rug at some time in the past. In 1993 the front portion of a large cat skull was found on Exmoor. It too eventually made its way to the Natural History Museum which confirmed it was from a mounted trophy.

Can a black domestic cat really have been mistaken for a black leopard?

Since a peak of sightings and other evidence in 1995 odd sightings of big black cats have continued to the present day both in the south Bodmin area and throughout much of Cornwall generally.

There is one final point to mention about the Beast of Bodmin. The MP for North Cornwall, Paul Tyler, has been very keen to encourage the government to hold enquiries and investigations into the reports to try to establish just what animals are present. He has made the point on several occasions that any animal found should be referred to as the 'Beast of Bodmin Moor', not the 'Beast of Bodmin'. Apparently his constituents in Bodmin are fed up with being referred to as beasts!

The Abyssinian Cat of south Cornwall

This is a classic tale of a well-meant misidentification. It attracted a phenomenal volume of media attention and became an ongoing mystery that was finally solved, in as much secrecy as it started, almost two and a half years later.

The story started on Thursday 27 November 1997 with a report in the *Cornish Guardian* covering most of the front page.

Beneath the headline 'The sunbathing Cornish puma' was a rather nice picture of a large Abyssinian domestic cat and a tabby, possibly a friend, curled up asleep behind him. The *Western Morning News* and the *Evening Herald* the following day both carried the same picture, again as a front page feature.

The Abyssinian cat was supposed to have been seen regularly in a village near St Austell and had been photographed by a local man who wanted the location kept secret. The *Cornish Guardian* editor, Alan Cooper, was keen to keep the location and identity of the photographer secret as well, in order further to protect the animal. He was convinced the pictures were genuine. Various experts who had been interviewed identified the cat as a female puma; at least one stated she was possibly pregnant! In the *Evening Herald* other experts used the opportunity to claim that pumas were living in the Plymouth area too, and coming right up to the outskirts of the city.

A quick council of war at work, and Paul Crowther (photographic lecturer and friend) and I sent a two-page press release to the *Cornish Guardian* and every other newspaper that had carried the story. We gave a reasoned argument why the animal shown was almost certainly a large domestic cat. Paul queried several technical characteristics of the picture, and I listed certain fairly straightforward biological facts which suggested it was not a puma, nor any other large mysterious exotic cat. The response was a very quick rebuttal, but we were invited to the *Cornish Guardian* office where we were shown another photograph the paper had not published for fear of revealing the location.

Whilst Alan Cooper and his deputy editor still did not wish to make known the location, we did obtain from them a few more facts and a simple explanation about why the photograph was slightly out of focus and had something of an odd, distorted appearance. The photographer had used a fairly elementary camera without a tele-photo lens, and to get a closer view he had taken the shot through a pair of binoculars!

Another advantage of seeing the unpublished picture was that it also showed a concrete block wall which gave us an idea of scale, and we were able to calculate that the size of the so-called puma was that of a large domestic cat. After we left the office we wrote a vaguely conciliatory letter to the *Cornish Guardian*, again commenting on the integrity of the editor, who in turn believed totally in the honesty of the photographer.

Everything then died down for a couple of years, except when further big cat sightings in Cornwall were reported and the same pictures were usually dragged out to be used in the local newspapers.

Two years later, Paul and I assisted Carlton Television in making a half-hour documentary called 'Tracking the beast', which was transmitted on 28 December 1999. Surprised at how much publicity the programme attracted, the college which employed us suggested we organise a mystery cat event for 'science week' in March 2000. Having thought about this, we decided a conference on the subject might be a good idea. The college allowed us to proceed, using our existing media contacts to publicise it.

After issuing a news release we were astounded to read within days that there was to be a 'major conference' with 'world experts' speaking. In truth the press were pretty eager to get hold of any cat stories at the time, because a few days earlier two animal keepers in Birmingham had admitted releasing both pumas and panthers in Derbyshire in the 1970s, and any local slant or story was desperately needed.

Almost as soon as the conference was announced the telephone started ringing. We had calls from radio stations and newspapers requesting interviews, and from people from all over Devon and Cornwall wanting either to book places or to report sightings. It was at this time that Paul received a call about the 'sunbathing Cornish puma' from two years previously.

Puma. This one is at Newquay Zoo, but they could survive in the wild in Devon and Cornwall

His conversation was most interesting: the owners of a large Abyssinian cat, somewhere on the coast of south Cornwall, were becoming increasingly fed up seeing their pet in the newspaper every time there was a 'Beast of Bodmin' or similar story. Apparently a neighbour had taken the pictures in the belief that the animal was one of Cornwall's big cats. We were sworn to secrecy, but Paul was given a location which he confirmed with the *Cornish Guardian*. Well, they didn't actually confirm it, but Paul was asked how on earth he had discovered it – or words to that effect!

The Abyssinian is one of the larger breeds of domestic cat and its coat colour can match that of the puma, so misidentification at a distance might not be quite so daft as it sounds. On the night of the conference, after he had shown the picture, Paul announced he had information from someone who wished to remain anonymous but who believed they owned the cat. The photographer, who we do not think was present, protested anonymously in the letters column of the *Cornish Guardian* the following week. But the cat was already out of the bag, so to speak…

The China Fleet Leopard

The China Fleet Club at Saltash is a rather nice golf and country club situated just to the north of the town and bordering the banks of the river Tamar. On 2 September 1994 it dramatically entered cat folk-lore with a multiple sighting by nine or ten people, the majority of whom were police officers.

At about 11 o'clock in the morning three separate groups of golfers watched a black, 1.8 metre (five foot) long cat with a thick tail walk across the golf course. At least one of these groups was made up of members of the East Cornwall police golf society.

Quite by chance a week later the Plymouth *Evening Herald* ran an article of mine on the presence of exotic cats in Devon and Cornwall, and after reading it the club manager, David O'Sullivan, gave me a call and asked me to come and have a look at the area where the cat had been seen.

As an ex-Royal Marine with a firm interest in nature, as well as golf, David took walks about the golf course as a regular and enjoyable part of his duties. When I arrived at the club, I was shown video footage he had taken of suspicious footprints in the bunkers. Whilst many of them were obviously those of domestic dogs and cats, we did find that some of the larger ones were of a size and appearance consistent with a big cat. Other circumstantial evidence also came to light: the rabbit population had dropped considerably in the last few weeks, and rabbits' back legs had been discovered, just bitten off and left, around the site.

Over the next nine months or so David telephoned me regularly to give an up-date on sightings. The media were not informed of all of them to avoid attracting big-game hunters, and in fact David gave a direction to his ground staff effectively banning firearms. What was interesting was that the sightings were often about 28-35 days apart. This is the typical time a puma or leopard might spend travelling around its range.

The sightings were often reported by people who had driven long distances to play on the course and who were not aware of the previous cat sightings (one or two made it clear that had they known about them they would not have played there). All reports were of a large black cat, and many regulars who publicly stated they did not believe in these animals carried cameras in their golf bags. Some players spent less time than usual looking for balls that had rolled into the rough!

Whilst investigating the China Fleet sightings I became aware of a number of other reports from the area immediately to the north of Saltash. After some time the China Fleet sightings became rarer and further apart, but then I received reports from near Pillaton (a charming village about 6 km (4 miles) north-west of Saltash). The late 1990s also provided evidence from around Kit Hill, immediately north of Pillaton.

This whole series of sightings is one of the more convincing I have looked into. An animal appeared on a regular basis in one part of a range, and then seemed to move into a more remote area as it matured. It could indeed therefore have been a leopard.

The Wrangaton Lion

This story starts on Thursday 19 November 1998, or at least it appears to – as with most of the big cat reports, if you investigate for long enough earlier reports often surface in or near the area in question. The sightings on this particular morning were taken very seriously and made front page headlines the following day in both the *Western Morning News* and the *Evening Herald*.

At about 9.15 am Paul Gourley was driving between Wrangaton and South Brent when he saw a male lion, with blood on its mane, run along a country lane in front of his car and then jump through a hedge. He got within 20 metres (22 yards) of it at one point. At around 11am two workmen saw a creature they believed to be a big cat in a field near Marley Cross, about 5 km (3 miles) to the east of the first sighting.

The media, keepers from the local zoo, and Devon and Cornwall constabulary (including the firearms unit) attended in force. At one stage a convoy of twenty vehicles was moving through the south Dartmoor countryside. None, of course, saw the animal. Casts of

Lions in Africa, male standing, female lying down. Lions are social animals, unlike most cats

footprints were taken by the staff of the Dartmoor Wildlife Park, who confirmed they were cat-like and larger than the puma prints already in their possession.

By Saturday of the same week the police were advising local gun owners not to try to kill the animal. Meanwhile, other sightings were being reported in the area, and it became apparent that suspicious footprints had been left in the bunkers at Wrangaton golf course a few weeks earlier.

The following year on 19 April, Len Ash and a friend were driving between Wrangaton and Bittaford at 11.30 am. The driver identified an animal crossing the road in front of them as a lion. When he reversed, his passenger saw it too and later stated it was 'a lion or a puma'. The police were called straight away, and an armed response unit and the force helicopter attended. The helicopter was fitted with a thermal imaging camera, and after hovering over the area for a few minutes it located a heat source in a copse. This was videoed, but seemed to disappear.

When the officers on the ground were directed to where the animal had supposedly been they found themselves in the middle of what was thought to be a live badger set. Various experts discussed the video footage on the news that night, but no absolute identification was possible.

A further reported sighting occurred on the evening of 4 May at Wrangaton when Sebastian Pope disturbed a large cat when he went to feed his chickens. The following morning an animal was seen on the eastern outskirts of Ivybridge, some 5 km (3 miles) to the west of Wrangaton. A fishmonger had been on his way to work when he saw a cat holding a lamb's carcase in its mouth while the other sheep in the field were panicking. Devon County Council issued a request that any further sightings should be reported to the police, and suggested that local children should be accompanied to and from school by an adult.

The reports were suddenly put into question though, when on 12 May the *Western Morning News* printed a letter from Mrs Kate Van Der Kiste of South Brent. On 19 November and 19 April she had been walking Rex, a very well built golden retriever, in the areas where the sightings had taken place. Apparently, it had been suggested previously that while walking in the woods Rex did rather look like a lion!

The sightings in the East Ivybridge vicinity continued over the summer, however, and no further mention of Rex's presence was hinted at. There was an allegation of a sheep kill at Smithaleigh in mid-October, and another sighting was made at Cornwood at the end of the month.

In fact sightings of cats in the south Dartmoor area had been recorded for some considerable time before this. The first reports were from Holbeton and Yealmpton (less than 13km or 8 miles from Wrangaton) in September and October 1966. One of the people who had seen the animal had even visited Plymouth Zoo later to

With all due respect to Rex, the very well-built golden retriever from South Brent, it seems unlikely he could be seriously mistaken for a lion such as this magnificent example

look at the pumas there and make comparisons. He confirmed he had seen a puma in the wild.

These reports were taken so seriously that the following year the great naturalist H G Hurrell included them in his annual report for the Devonshire Association. The *Western Morning News* of 14 June 1967 carried an article about his report but when the *Transactions of the Devonshire Association* were later published the puma sightings were omitted. At the time particular credence was given to the reports, because two sightings had been by Commander R Mildmay-White of Mothecombe. Possibly even more surprising was the letter a few days later, again in the *Western Morning News*, by a man from Crownhill in Plymouth who claimed to have seen a puma in the grounds of the Royal Naval Engineering College at Manadon, Plymouth, on two or three occasions!

Interestingly the *Transactions of the Devonshire Association* did publish reports of both 'black panthers' and 'pumas' in their 1971 edition. However, they were not in the mammal section, as might be expected, but in the folklore report. This referred to sightings which came from all over Devon from the previous April onwards.

When the conference on 'The Beast' took place at Plymouth College of Further Education, one of the speakers was Ellis Daw, the owner and director of Dartmoor Wildlife Park at Sparkwell. This is one of the few zoological collections in the United Kingdom still to have pumas. Ellis confined his short talk to his observation of wild pumas in the area. Both he and several members of his staff had seen them in the outer boundaries of the park, and on one occasion actually sniffing around the outside of the puma enclosure.

Sparkwell is about 10 km (6 miles) away from Wrangaton, across fairly wild countryside on the moorland edge. It would seem the area is particularly big cat friendly – typical sightings are of a brown puma-type animal, and as far as I am aware no large, leopard-type cats have been glimpsed.

Conclusions

Ignoring the more 'suspicious' reports, the number of sightings of large cats, both black and brown, throughout Devon and Cornwall is still large enough for there to be really little doubt about these animals' existence. If the recent sightings are recorded on a map, outlines of likely territories are revealed:

1. South Dartmoor, from the edges of Plympton and Plymstock east round the edges of Cornwood and Ivybridge, on to Wrangaton and some distance further out to the east.

2. East Cornwall, from just north of Saltash (the China Fleet club), up the edge of the river Tamar and inland as far as the St Mellion golf course and Pillaton, possibly up to Kit Hill.

3. The edge of Exmoor to the south and west, in a band from South Molton to Coombe Martin.

4. The southern edge of Bodmin Moor, from Common Moor (near Siblyback Reservoir) up to Jamaica Inn.

5. A band stretching from Falmouth to Penzance.

6. A band heading north from St Austell to Lanivet.

While a few sightings have happened outside these loosely defined areas, over the last thirty or so years the bulk of sightings and other evidence have come from within them. Some of these have been discredited, either as hoaxes or genuine mistakes, but in every case a backbone of very believable evidence survives.

The territories provide an ideal habitat for the animals and they are each sufficiently large to produce enough wildlife to feed a big solitary predator such as a puma or leopard without it having to take domestic livestock regularly. Should domestic livestock be killed for prey, the numbers are likely to be insignificant when compared with those killed by dogs, lack of veterinary care and, in the case of high moorland during the winter, exposure.

If the cats we are considering are the descendants (between the third and seventh generations) of animals that were released in the mid-1970s, then they must be approaching a stable population.

If this is the case, there is a good chance of them becoming permanently established. However, their comparatively small numbers would still be vulnerable to a particularly virulent cat disease either through all of them succumbing directly or through reduced groups being unable to sustain a breeding population.

The future

If we assume that we have pumas, and possibly black leopards, living in Devon and Cornwall, and we follow the popular notion that they are the descendants of animals released around 1976, we can assume that we now have a viable breeding population. Subject to that population not being seriously reduced by disease we can also assume it will continue to increase.

Greater numbers will inevitably result in more sightings and possibly more conflict with domestic livestock. Conversely it could be argued that as the numbers of deer and rabbits rise and agriculture becomes geared more towards crop growing than meat and dairy farming, the large cats will actually be beneficial to the farming community. As far as humans are concerned, for the forseeable future they pose only a very small risk – according to statistics bees, wasps, dogs and cattle probably pose a greater threat in the short term.

At the time of printing there have been no serious attacks on people by exotic cats living wild in the UK, and most of the alleged attacks that have taken place have attracted some comment as to their veracity. This is mainly because of the trivial nature and type of injuries caused or, in at least one case, local knowledge of the behaviour and habits of the victim.

If a serious human attack does occur in the future, there will be an obvious call for the animal's capture or destruction. This will presumably be delegated to the local police who will, in turn, be offered help and advice from various other agencies.

Practically all that can be done at present is to try to keep a record of all the sightings and evidence for the existence of these animals. There is currently no national recording system, and to establish one without the facilities of a government department or a major academic institution is probably not feasible. In virtually every county, however, there are amateur recorders who have the advantage of local knowledge of geography, biology, and sometimes of the personalities reporting the sightings and associated evidence.

Although the police have in the past reacted to reports, they do not have a legal obligation to do so except where there is an issue of public safety, or an indication of an offence having been committed. As the evidence so far is that neither of these circumstances seems to apply, it is likely the police will respond less and less to sightings, which tends to bring the focus back on to the amateur private researcher.

The downside of this is that amateur researchers do tend to change address and often lose interest after a few years. One or two are known to have given up because of regular attentions by hoaxers. So, possibly the best course of action an eyewitness can take is to contact the local zoological gardens. Most of the zoos, even if they do not have the time or interest to follow up the report themselves, are aware of whoever is currently recording the animals in the area. In addition they are unlikely to pass on information to anyone who would wish to harm the animals.

If the existence of these large predators is proved beyond doubt and their numbers continue to increase, Devon and Cornwall, albeit unwittingly, will enter one of the greatest repopulation experiments in modern times. The fact that the founder individuals appear to have become established as a result of accidental or intentional secret releases makes the whole phenomenon even more fascinating.

Further reading

ADAS, *The evidence for the presence of large exotic cats in the Bodmin area and their possible impact on livestock* (MAFF Publications, 1995, London)

Beer, T, *The Beast of Exmoor: Fact or Legend?* (Countryside Productions, 1988, Barnstaple, a title now distributed by Tor Mark Press)

Brierly, N, *They stalk by Night – the big cats of Exmoor and the South West* (Yeo Valley Productions, 1988, Bishops Nympton)

Downes, J, *The Smaller Mystery Carnivores of the Westcountry* (CFZ, 1996, Exeter)

Francis, D, *Cat Country* (David and Charles, 1983, Newton Abbot)

Francis, D, *The Beast of Exmoor and other mystery predators of Britain* (Jonathan Cape, 1993, London)

Shuker, K, *Mystery cats of the world* (Robert Hale, 1989, London)

For up to date information many of the local newspapers, such as the *Western Morning News, Cornish Guardian* and *Herald Express*, have internet web sites. Some have archive search features, meaning that searches can be made over the last couple of years using key words.

A number of private researchers have informative and detailed websites as well. The addresses of these do change regularly, but they usually link to each other. If you use a search engine and specify key words such as 'Beast of Bodmin' a number can usually be found quite quickly.